Welcome, Fellow Lovescaper!

In this workbook, you will find a personal space to work on your Lovescaping skills. You can think of it as a guide and a journal for you to learn, take action and reflect on your practice of the pillars of Lovescaping. We encourage you to be creative and make this workbook your own by using your unique and preferred communication style, whether it's through writing, scribbling, drawing, poetry, doodling, etc. You can also include questions you may have that come up as you put these pillars into practice!

Examples of communication styles you can use in your workbook:

TABLE OF CONTENTS

01 Glossary of Terms

02 How to Use this Workbook

03 Questions

04 Introduction to Lovescaping

07 Triggers & Self-Regulation

10 Humility	**25** Compassion	**40** Solidarity
13 Empathy	**28** Patience	**43** Liberation
16 Respect	**31** Honesty	**46** Gratitude
19 Communication	**34** Vulnerability	**49** Forgiveness
22 Care	**37** Trust	**52** Hope

55 Final Reflection

Glossary of TERMS

DEFINITION: the meaning and description of the topic or Lovescaping pillar at the beginning of each section.

LOVESCAPER: a practitioner of the 15 pillars of Lovescaping.

PILLAR OF LOVESCAPING: one of the key components to practice love in action. There are 15 in total.

OBJECTIVES: the desired goals or learning outcomes for each of the topics and pillars.

PRACTICE: a section where you can put the learned skill or pillar into practice by working through a scenario.

REFLECTION: a space where you can think deeply and reflect on your practice of the skill and pillar.

SELF-EVALUATION: a space where you can assess yourself and take responsibility for your practice of the pillar.

SMART GOAL: when setting goals for your life, remember to make them SMART! This will make it more likely for you to accomplish them:

- *Specific:* make your goal as detailed and specific as possible.
- *Measurable:* make sure you'll be able to quantify or measure your goal.
- *Actionable:* make sure there are specific actions you can take to achieve your goal.
- *Realistic:* make sure your goal is something you can actually do; that's why it needs to be realistic.
- *Time-bound:* make sure your goal has a specific time frame or deadline.

PILLAR OF THE WEEK
Activities to practice and review all 15 pillars of Lovescaping.

How To Use This WORKBOOK

This workbook is divided into 17 sections that correspond to the introduction of Lovescaping, self-regulation, and 15 pillars. You will find under each "Pillar of the Week" the same format and activities to work through. The goal is for you to use the workbook to reflect, practice, and solidify what you're learning during the Lovescaping sessions.

Remember to make this workbook your own and be creative!

Under each section you will find:

1 **Objectives**
Reflect on your own childhood and think about things you'd like to change or improve to make things better by answering some questions.

2 **Definition**
Review the definition of the Lovescaping pillar and a few examples.

3 **In Your Own Words**
Practice giving that pillar your own definition. Remember that you are free to write, draw, or express your idea however you want.

4 **Practice**
Think of a situation or scenario from your own life where you can put each skill and pillar into practice.

5 **Goal setting**
You will set your own SMART goal for the week to practice that skill/pillar in your life.

6 **Reflection & Self-Evaluation**
- You will answer some questions, reflect on your SMART goal and think about how you can improve.
- You will reflect on the relationship between and among all the pillars of Lovescaping.

QUESTIONS

> Use this section to write down any questions or thoughts you have to bring back to your next session or for you to further explore.

Introduction to LOVESCAPING

OBJECTIVES

- Define love, intentionality and unlearning in your own words.
- Apply intentionality and unlearning to a situation in your life.
- Set a goal for practicing intentionality and unlearning this week.
- Reflect on the concepts of intentionally, unlearning and love in action.
- Take Action! Share how you practiced intentionality, unlearning and love in action this week.

DEFINITION

Lovescaping is practicing love in action through the intentional and purposeful engagement of its 15 pillars:

empathy, compassion, solidarity, humility, honesty, gratitude, communication, care, forgiveness, patience, liberation, trust, vulnerability, respect, and hope.

Lovescaping requires us to unlearn where necessary in order to be intentional about practicing the pillars in our lives. *Unlearning* is the process of letting go of previously held beliefs, assumptions, and habits that may no longer be useful or accurate. Unlearning can be difficult because it often requires us to confront our own biases and question long-held assumptions, but it can also be a powerful tool for personal and professional growth. Intentionality is being purposeful and deliberate in one's actions, thoughts, and decisions. The more intentional we become about unlearning and learning, the more self-aware we become.

Example of unlearning:
You realize you learned in your childhood to suppress feelings and not share them with others. You begin the process of unlearning and learning how to share your feelings with your children.

Example of intentionality:
Every night before going to bed, you ask your family members to put their phones away and sit together to talk about what went well during the day and what was challenging.

IN YOUR OWN WORDS

What is your definition of **love**, **intentionality** and **unlearning**?

_____
_____
_____
_____
_____
_____
_____
_____

PRACTICE

Think of a situation in your own life where you can practice unlearning and intentionality. How can you apply these concepts to love?

GOAL SETTING

What is one SMART goal you will set this week to practice unlearning and/or intentionality?

EXAMPLE:

This week, I will practice intentionality by playing a 5-minute guided meditation every night before going to sleep. I will practice unlearning by replacing my negative thought "I can't do it" with "Yes, I can!" every time it pops up in my mind.

My goal for practicing intentionality and/or unlearning this week:

_____
_____
_____

REFLECTION - SELF-EVALUATION

- Did you accomplish your goal/s?

- Why or why not?

- How will you continue practicing intentionality and unlearning? What are your next steps? Write two actions for improving:

  1.

  2.

- Why do you think **intentionality** and **unlearning** are necessary to practice love in action?

TRIGGERS & SELF-REGULATION

OBJECTIVES

- *Define self-regulation in your own words and identify your triggers.*
- *Apply self-regulation to a situation in your life.*
- *Set a goal for practicing self-regulation this week.*
- *Reflect on why self-regulation is necessary to practice the pillars of Lovescaping.*
- *Take Action! Share how you practiced self-regulation this week.*

DEFINITION

Self-regulation is a learned skill that allows you to understand and manage your emotions, behavior and responses to feelings and situations happening around you. We feel our emotions in our bodies. When we are triggered, our bodies are dysregulated. When we operate from this state, we are more likely to do or say something we regret. Our goal is to get to a regulated state so we can respond from a place of love and not fear or anger.

Example of self-regulation:

 Your teenage daughter is late (again!) and you start getting angry.

 You take deep breaths before sending her a text message.

07

IN YOUR OWN WORDS

How can you define **self-regulation** in your own words?

_____
_____
_____
_____
_____
_____
_____
_____

PRACTICE

Think of a situation in your own life where you can practice self-regulation. What triggers you? Which self-regulation strategy can you use? You can think of a past experience where you didn't practice self-regulation. How would you do it differently?

- What triggered you?
  _____
- How did you respond?
  _____
- How did that response make you feel?
  _____

What is the Lovescaping way?
_____
_____
_____

GOAL SETTING

What is one SMART goal you will set this week to practice self-regulation?

EXAMPLE:

This week, I will practice self-regulation by taking a sip of water when my body becomes dysregulated when my child ignores my questions so I can respond instead of react.

My goal for practicing self-regulation this week:

_____

_____

_____

REFLECTION - SELF-EVALUATION

- Did you accomplish your goal/s?

- Why or why not?

- How will you continue practicing self-regulation? What are your next steps? Write two actions for improving:

    1.

    2.

- Why do you think **self-regulation** is necessary to practice love in action?

OBJECTIVES

- Define humility in your own words.
- Apply humility to a situation in your life.
- Set a goal for practicing humility this week.
- Reflect on why humility is necessary to practice the pillars of Lovescaping.
- Take Action! Share how you practiced humility this week.

HUMILITY

DEFINITION

Humility is understanding that you are not above or below others, better or worse than others, but rather, you see yourself as a human being on the same plain, just different. When we practice humility, we understand that we do not know everything, open ourselves to learning, admit our mistakes, and accept others. When you practice humility, you are humble, and you are free from pride or arrogance.

Examples of humility:

- You are patient.
- You admit mistakes.
- You have an open mind.
- You embrace differences.
- You find value in everyone.
- You take responsibility.
- You are a good team player.
- You are open to learning from new ideas.
- You listen to others and try to understand them.
- You want others around you to succeed.

Humility in Action

 You had a difficult day at work and when you got home, your child asked you for help with their homework. You snap and yell: "You can't do anything by yourself!" You go to your room and immediately regret your words. You take a few deep breaths and call your child in: "I am so sorry about what I said to you. That wasn't true. I had a tough day at work and I unloaded it all on you. Can you forgive me?"

10

IN YOUR OWN WORDS

How can you define **humility** in your own words?

_____
_____
_____
_____
_____
_____
_____

PRACTICE

Think of a situation in your own life where you can practice humility more intentionally. This can be a past experience where you didn't practice humility. How would you do it differently?

What triggered you?	**What is the Lovescaping way?**
_____	_____
How did you respond?	_____
_____	_____
How did that response make you feel?	_____
_____	_____

GOAL SETTING

What is one SMART goal you will set this week to practice humility?

EXAMPLE:

This week, I will practice humility by spending 15 minutes every evening watching the "Human" documentary on YouTube with my teenage son to learn about different perspectives and experiences from humans around the world.

My goal for practicing humility this week:

_____

_____

_____

REFLECTION - SELF-EVALUATION

- Did you accomplish your goal/s?

- Why or why not?

- How will you continue practicing humility? What are your next steps? Write two actions for improving:
  1.
  2.

- Why do you think **humility** is one of the pillars of Lovescaping?

OBJECTIVES

- Define empathy in your own words.
- Set a goal for practicing empathy this week.
- Reflect on the importance of putting empathy into practice.
- Reflect on why empathy is one of the pillars of Lovescaping.
- Take Action! Share how you practiced empathy this week.

EMPATHY

DEFINITION

Empathy is the ability to understand and share the feelings of another person. It means putting yourself in someone else's shoes to see how things look and feel from someone's situation or perspective. Here are some questions you can ask yourself and work on to build your empathy skills: Can I identify the emotions in others? What are they communicating with their words and body language? How would I feel if it was me? What can I say to show that I care? You are empathetic when you understand and share the feelings of another person.

Examples of empathy:

- ✓ You listen deeply with the goal of understanding and not responding.
- ✓ You imagine how you would feel if you were in that situation.
- ✓ You understand that every behavior is a form of communication.
- ✓ You can identify the emotions in another person.
- ✓ You support and care about others.
- ✓ You show kindness.
- ✓ You don't judge.

Empathy in Action

 Your daughter comes back from school and tells you she's feeling sad because her friends didn't invite her to play during recess. You say: "I see you are sad and upset, honey. It's hurtful when you are left out. I'm sorry that happened, tell me more about how it made you feel. I'm here for you."

IN YOUR OWN WORDS

How can you define **empathy** in your own words?

_____
_____
_____
_____
_____
_____
_____

PRACTICE

Think of a situation in your own life where you can practice empathy more intentionally. This can be a past experience where you didn't practice empathy. How would you do it differently?

What triggered you?	**What is the Lovescaping way?**
_____	_____
How did you respond?	
_____	_____
How did that response make you feel?	
_____	_____

GOAL SETTING

What is one SMART goal you will set this week to practice empathy?

EXAMPLE:

This week, I will practice empathy every day during dinner by asking my daughter what went well and what was challenging during her day. I will listen actively and will connect with her feelings instead of jumping to advice.

My goal for practicing empathy this week:

_____

_____

_____

REFLECTION - SELF-EVALUATION

- Did you accomplish your goal/s?

- Why or why not?

- How will you continue practicing empathy? What are your next steps? Write two actions for improving:

    1.

    2.

- Why do you think **empathy** is one of the pillars of Lovescaping?

OBJECTIVES

- Define respect in your own words.
- Set a goal for practicing respect this week.
- Reflect on the importance of putting respect into practice.
- Reflect on why respect is one of the pillars of Lovescaping.
- Take Action! Share how you practiced respect this week.

RESPECT

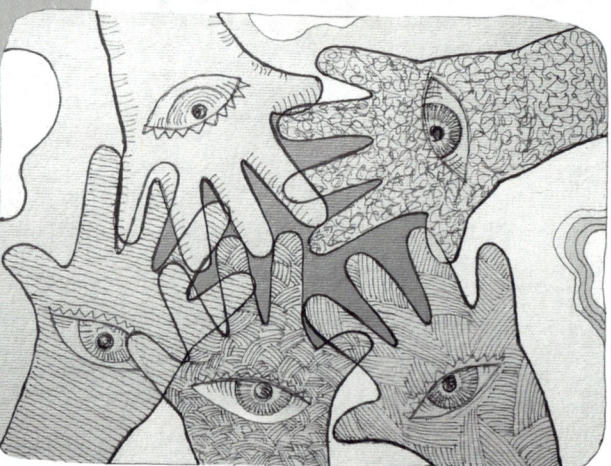

DEFINITION

Respect is valuing and accepting ourselves and others, treating one another with dignity. We respect when we give value, listen and recognize another person's voice, point of view, and lived experience. We show respect with our words, body language, and actions. When we respect, we accept people for who they are, without judging them or trying to change them.

Examples of respect:

- ☑ You don't interrupt.
- ☑ You learn from others.
- ☑ You make eye contact.
- ☑ You wait for your turn patiently.
- ☑ You use words such as "please" and "thank you."
- ☑ You make a person feel comfortable and safe.
- ☑ You listen to someone when they are talking.
- ☑ You listen to other people's opinions and beliefs, even if you disagree.
- ☑ You communicate using "I" messages.
- ☑ You use your words and body language to show that you are paying attention.

Respect in Action

Your son is telling you about his soccer practice at school while you are on your phone texting and resolving a problem with a family member. You put your phone down and make eye contact with your child and say to him: "I wasn't showing you respect by being on my phone while you were talking to me. You have my attention now, please tell me about it."

IN YOUR OWN WORDS

How can you define **respect** in your own words?

_____
_____
_____
_____
_____
_____
_____

PRACTICE

Think of a situation in your own life where you can practice respect more intentionally. This can be a past experience where you didn't practice respect. How would you do it differently?

What triggered you?	**What is the Lovescaping way?**
_____	_____
How did you respond?	
_____	_____
How did that response make you feel?	
_____	_____

GOAL SETTING

What is one SMART goal you will set this week to practice respect?

EXAMPLE:

This week, I will practice respect with my son every evening. I will put my phone away for 20 minutes to ask him questions about his day, listen to him with interest, make eye contact and ask follow-up questions.

My goal for practicing respect this week:

_____
_____
_____

REFLECTION - SELF-EVALUATION

- Did you accomplish your goal/s?

- Why or why not?

- How will you continue practicing respect? What are your next steps? Write two actions for improving:
  1.
  2.

- Why do you think **respect** is one of the pillars of Lovescaping?

OBJECTIVES

COMMUNICATION

- Define communication in your own words.
- Set a goal for practicing communication this week.
- Reflect on the importance of putting communication into practice.
- Reflect on why communication is one of the pillars of Lovescaping.
- Take Action! Share how you practiced communication this week.

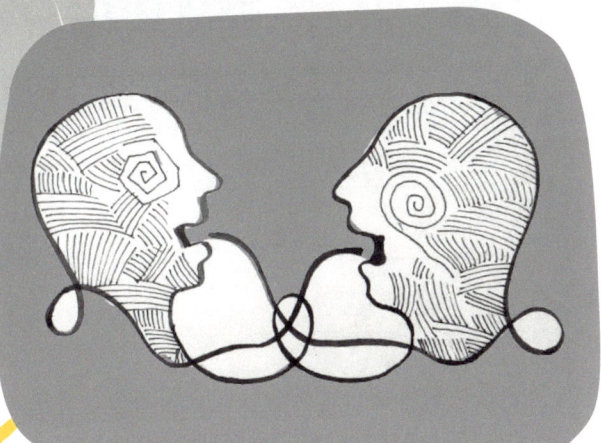

DEFINITION

Communication is the process by which we transmit our thoughts, feelings, and emotions through different mediums. We constantly communicate, exchanging information, and addressing each other in verbal and non-verbal ways. Communication is the basis of any relationship. Our ability to communicate allows us to survive, grow, and develop.

Examples of communication:

- ☑ You listen to others respectfully.
- ☑ You use words to resolve conflict.
- ☑ You don't make assumptions.
- ☑ You make eye contact when speaking to others.
- ☑ You use your body language appropriately.
- ☑ You ask questions when you don't understand something.
- ☑ You ask questions before you assume something.
- ☑ You use "I" statements to communicate your thoughts, feelings and needs.

Communication in Action

Your child tells you he got a low grade on his science project, and he doesn't understand why. You say to him: "can you tell me more about what happened? Did you talk to your teacher about it?" Your child responds: "No, I thought they didn't like my project." You say: "before making assumptions, let's gather all the information. Maybe you can schedule a time to speak with your teacher and ask for feedback. I'm here to support you through this."

IN YOUR OWN WORDS

How can you define **communication** in your own words?

_____
_____
_____
_____
_____
_____
_____
_____

PRACTICE

Think of a situation in your own life where you can practice communication more intentionally. This can be a past experience where you didn't practice communication. How would you do it differently?

What triggered you?	What is the Lovescaping way?
_____	_____
How did you respond?	
_____	_____
How did that response make you feel?	
_____	_____

GOAL SETTING

What is one SMART goal you will set this week to practice communication?

EXAMPLE:

This week, I will practice Nonviolent Communication (NVC) while having breakfast with my children by being intentional about using "I" statements instead of using sentences that start with "You" and resorting to blaming and pointing fingers.

My goal for practicing communication this week:

_____
_____
_____

REFLECTION - SELF-EVALUATION

- Did you accomplish your goal/s?

- Why or why not?

- How will you continue practicing communication? What are your next steps? Write two actions for improving:

    1.

    2.

- Why do you think **communication** is one of the pillars of Lovescaping?

OBJECTIVES

- Define care in your own words.
- Set a goal for practicing care this week.
- Reflect on the importance of putting care into practice.
- Reflect on why care is one of the pillars of Lovescaping.
- Take Action! Share how you practiced care this week.

CARE

DEFINITION

Care is giving time and attention to and looking after things or people that matter to us with kindness and affection. We show that we care about others by being consistent, reliable, and trustworthy. The most precious gift we can give someone to show that we care is our time. Self-Care is directing that attention, kindness and affection towards ourselves. Self-Care is any activity you do to take care of your mental, physical, and emotional health.

Examples of care:

- You spend quality time with people you love.
- You do an act of kindness for someone else.
- You call friends and family who are far away.
- You do things that make you happy.
- You help people when they need it.
- You hug the people you love.
- You notice people in your day to day and ask how they are doing.
- You spend time with people who make you feel good about yourself.
- You keep your word. If you make a promise, you own it. If you make a commitment, you stick to it.
- You eat healthy foods and exercise regularly.

Care in Action

You say to your son: "How about we plan some quality time together this weekend? Any ideas on what you'd like to do?" Your son says: "Can we go to the park and fly a kite, Mom?" You say: "That's a fantastic idea! We can pack a picnic lunch and spend the whole afternoon there. It'll be a fun opportunity to bond and enjoy each other's company. I'm looking forward to spending quality time with you, sweetheart."

22

IN YOUR OWN WORDS

How can you define **care** in your own words?

_____
_____
_____
_____
_____
_____
_____

PRACTICE

Think of a situation in your own life where you can practice care more intentionally. This can be a past experience where you didn't practice care. How would you do it differently?

What triggered you?	**What is the Lovescaping way?**
_____	_____
How did you respond?	
_____	_____
How did that response make you feel?	
_____	_____

GOAL SETTING

What is one SMART goal you will set this week to practice care?

EXAMPLE:

This week, I will practice self-care by listening to a 10-minute guided meditation every night before going to bed.

My goal for practicing care this week:

_____
_____
_____

REFLECTION - SELF-EVALUATION

- Did you accomplish your goal/s?

- Why or why not?

- How will you continue practicing care? What are your next steps? Write two actions for improving:
  1.
  2.

- Why do you think **care** is one of the pillars of Lovescaping?

24

OBJECTIVES

- Define compassion in your own words.
- Set a goal for practicing compassion this week.
- Reflect on the importance of putting compassion into practice.
- Reflect on why compassion is one of the pillars of Lovescaping.
- Take Action! Share how you practiced compassion this week.

COMPASSION

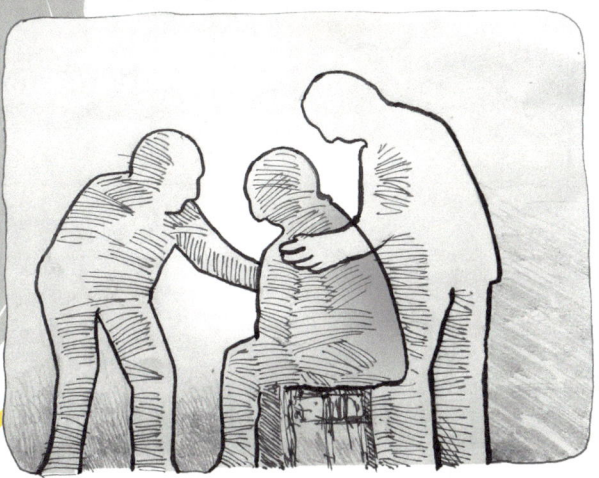

DEFINITION

Compassion means being able to share other people's suffering and feel with them. Being compassionate helps alleviate the suffering of those around us because we share it. When we are compassionate, we are letting others know they are not alone in their grief, that we care about them and that we are there to support them. Compassion is the foundation of humanity. When we lose our compassion, we risk losing our humanity. When we don't care about the suffering of others, it's easy to become indifferent and do nothing to help make things better. Compassion is necessary to take action and help heal our world!

Examples of compassion:

- ✓ You have felt sad when others are sad too.
- ✓ You notice when others are feeling sad.
- ✓ You reach out and provide support when others are sad.
- ✓ You embrace yourself with kindness and care when you are feeling sad.
- ✓ You act when someone is being mistreated.
- ✓ You listen to others when they are going through a difficult time.

Compassion in Action

There's a death in the family and your children are struggling with making sense of their loss. You say to them: "Let's process our grief together as a family. You can talk if you feel like talking, you can write a letter or draw a picture. You can choose a song that reminds you of our loved one, and we'll sit in the living room together and hold space for each other to be compassionate."

IN YOUR OWN WORDS

How can you define **compassion** in your own words?

_____
_____
_____
_____
_____
_____
_____
_____

PRACTICE

Think of a situation in your own life where you can practice compassion more intentionally. This can be a past experience where you didn't practice compassion. How would you do it differently?

What triggered you?	**What is the Lovescaping way?**
How did you respond?	
How did that response make you feel?	

GOAL SETTING

What is one SMART goal you will set this week to practice compassion?

EXAMPLE:

This week, I will prioritize self-compassion by setting aside 5 minutes each day to practice positive self-talk by replacing self-criticism with self-affirming statements.

My goal for practicing compassion this week:

_____

_____

_____

REFLECTION - SELF-EVALUATION

- Did you accomplish your goal/s?

- Why or why not?

- How will you continue practicing compassion? What are your next steps? Write two actions for improving:

  1.

  2.

- Why do you think **compassion** is one of the pillars of Lovescaping?

OBJECTIVES

- Define patience in your own words.
- Set a goal for practicing patience this week.
- Reflect on the importance of putting patience into practice.
- Reflect on why patience is one of the pillars of Lovescaping.
- Take Action! Share how you practiced patience this week.

PATIENCE

DEFINITION

Patience is allowing time for things to happen and develop without becoming agitated, upset, or losing our temper. The key to patience is realizing that most things that are important in this world require time. It takes time to develop trust, to learn, to understand, and ultimately to love. When you are patient, you understand and value the time that it takes to work on yourself, on relationships, on learning, and growing. Having patience helps you persevere and not give up.

Examples of patience:

- ☑ You don't get frustrated with others.
- ☑ You don't give up, and you try again.
- ☑ You wait for your turn to speak.
- ☑ You are empathetic with others.
- ☑ You keep working towards your goals.
- ☑ You have a good attitude while waiting for something.
- ☑ You put in the time it takes to learn new things.
- ☑ You take deep breaths whenever you start feeling impatient.

Patience in Action

You are at the post office with your children and there's a long line. They start complaining and getting frustrated. You say to them: "let's take a few deep breaths and do some grounding exercises with our 5 senses to patiently wait for our turn."

IN YOUR OWN WORDS

How can you define **patience** in your own words?

_____
_____
_____
_____
_____
_____
_____
_____

PRACTICE

Think of a situation in your own life where you can practice patience more intentionally. This can be a past experience where you didn't practice patience. How would you do it differently?

- What triggered you?
  _____
- How did you respond?
  _____
- How did that response make you feel?
  _____

What is the Lovescaping way?

_____
_____
_____

GOAL SETTING

What is one SMART goal you will set this week to practice patience?

EXAMPLE:

This week, I will practice patience by doing the square breathing exercise when I'm helping my children with their homework. When I start feeling frustrated, I will close my eyes and take 4 breaths before I say anything to them.

My goal for practicing patience this week:

_____
_____
_____

REFLECTION - SELF-EVALUATION

- Did you accomplish your goal/s?

- Why or why not?

- How will you continue practicing patience? What are your next steps? Write two actions for improving:

  1.

  2.

- Why do you think **patience** is one of the pillars of Lovescaping?

OBJECTIVES

- Define honesty in your own words.
- Set a goal for practicing honesty this week.
- Reflect on the importance of putting honesty into practice.
- Reflect on why honesty is one of the pillars of Lovescaping.
- Take Action! Share how you practiced honesty this week.

HONESTY

DEFINITION

Honesty is being truthful, open, and transparent. Honesty means speaking our truth to others, expressing our feelings, emotions, fears, dreams, doubts, and experiences. Honesty allows us to build authentic relationships based on our true selves. Being honest can be very difficult; it can even hurt at times, but it is necessary to build a solid relationship based on trust.

Examples of honesty:

- You behave with integrity: you do the right thing when no one is watching.
- You share how you really feel and what you really think.
- You are honest with yourself and seek help if you need it.
- You are respectful when you communicate honestly with others.
- You take responsibility for your actions.
- You stick to your promises and commitments.

Honesty in Action

Your son was tasked with doing the laundry after finishing his homework. When you get home from work he says: "Dad, I'm sorry, I haven't done the laundry because I got carried away playing computer games." You say: "Thank you for being honest with me, son. I appreciate your honesty. I'm a little disappointed because I was hoping you would follow through with your commitment, but it's important that you were truthful about it, instead of making excuses. Let's work together so you can manage your time better and finish your chores first before playing computer games. I value our trust and openness with each other, and I'm proud of you for taking responsibility.

IN YOUR OWN WORDS

How can you define **honesty** in your own words?

_____
_____
_____
_____
_____
_____
_____

PRACTICE

Think of a situation in your own life where you can practice honesty more intentionally. This can be a past experience where you didn't practice honesty. How would you do it differently?

- What triggered you?
  _____
- How did you respond?
  _____
- How did that response make you feel?
  _____

What is the Lovescaping way?

_____
_____
_____

GOAL SETTING

What is one SMART goal you will set this week to practice honesty?

EXAMPLE:

This week, I will practice honesty by spending 10 minutes every night before going to bed sharing a story with my children about a time when I was honest and a time when I lied in my past. I will share what I learned from these experiences and why honesty matters.

My goal for practicing honesty this week:

_____
_____
_____

REFLECTION - SELF-EVALUATION

- Did you accomplish your goal/s?

- Why or why not?

- How will you continue practicing honesty? What are your next steps? Write two actions for improving:

   1.

   2.

- Why do you think **honesty** is one of the pillars of Lovescaping?

OBJECTIVES

VULNERABILITY

- Define vulnerability in your own words.
- Set a goal for practicing vulnerability this week.
- Reflect on the importance of putting vulnerability into practice.
- Reflect on why vulnerability is one of the pillars of Lovescaping.
- Take Action! Share how you practiced vulnerability this week.

DEFINITION

Vulnerability is uncertainty, risk and emotional exposure. When we are vulnerable, we open our hearts and show our true selves. Vulnerability is courageous, and when we learn to be vulnerable with one another, we develop honesty, trust and build stronger relationships.

Examples of vulnerability:

- You take risks.
- You are okay with uncertainty.
- You share your pain and insecurities.
- You express and share all your feelings.
- You believe that expressing all your emotions is brave.
- You understand that nobody is perfect.
- You open up about the things that you are afraid of.

Vulnerability in Action

You tell your children: "I'm going to be vulnerable with you. Sometimes I feel insecure about myself. I try to pretend that I'm confident and I know what I'm doing, but inside I feel uncertain and doubt myself. It helps to say it aloud and I want you to know that it's okay if you feel that way sometimes. We are here to support each other!"

IN YOUR OWN WORDS

How can you define **vulnerability** in your own words?

_____
_____
_____
_____
_____
_____
_____
_____

PRACTICE

Think of a situation in your own life where you can practice vulnerability more intentionally. This can be a past experience where you didn't practice vulnerability. How would you do it differently?

	What is the Lovescaping way?
• What triggered you?	_____
• How did you respond?	_____
• How did that response make you feel?	_____

GOAL SETTING

What is one SMART goal you will set this week to practice vulnerability?

EXAMPLE:

This week, I will practice vulnerability with my children while having dinner by sharing an experience that made me feel ashamed and insecure.

My goal for practicing vulnerability this week:

_____
_____
_____

REFLECTION - SELF-EVALUATION

- Did you accomplish your goal/s?

- Why or why not?

- How will you continue practicing vulnerability? What are your next steps? Write two actions for improving:

    1.

    2.

- Why do you think **vulnerability** is one of the pillars of Lovescaping?

OBJECTIVES

- Define trust in your own words.
- Set a goal for practicing trust this week.
- Reflect on the importance of putting trust into practice.
- Reflect on why trust is one of the pillars of Lovescaping.
- Take Action! Share how you practiced trust this week.

TRUST

DEFINITION

Trust is the ability to believe sincerely in someone or something. It requires us to be vulnerable and honest and to let go of fear. Developing trust takes time. Trust is the consequence of being honest, caring, vulnerable, and communicative.

Examples of trust:

- ☑ You are reliable.
- ☑ You keep secrets.
- ☑ You keep your promises.
- ☑ You follow through with your commitments.
- ☑ You are honest.
- ☑ You have integrity.
- ☑ You are consistent.
- ☑ You don't give in to peer pressure.

Trust in Action

Your daughter asks if she can go on a weekend trip with her friends. You say: "After giving it some thought, I've decided to trust you to go on the trip with your friends. I trust that you will make responsible choices and follow the agreements we've set in place. However, I want you to check in with me regularly and keep me updated on your plans. Remember, my trust in you is not a given, but something you need to earn and maintain through your actions. I believe in you, and I'm proud of the responsible young woman you're becoming."

IN YOUR OWN WORDS

How can you define **trust** in your own words?

_____
_____
_____
_____
_____
_____
_____
_____

PRACTICE

Think of a situation in your own life where you can practice trust more intentionally. This can be a past experience where you didn't practice trust. How would you do it differently?

What triggered you?	**What is the Lovescaping way?**
_____	_____
How did you respond?	
_____	_____
How did that response make you feel?	
_____	_____

GOAL SETTING

What is one SMART goal you will set this week to practice trust?

EXAMPLE:

This week, I will practice trust with my children by delegating household tasks to them, including setting the table and organizing their belongings, and trust that they will complete these tasks responsibly. I will also involve them in decision-making processes, such as planning family outings or determining their own schedules, while providing guidance and support.

My goal for practicing trust this week:

_____

_____

_____

REFLECTION - SELF-EVALUATION

- Did you accomplish your goal/s?

- Why or why not?

- How will you continue practicing trust? What are your next steps? Write two actions for improving:

   1.

   2.

- Why do you think **trust** is one of the pillars of Lovescaping?

OBJECTIVES

- Define solidarity in your own words.
- Set a goal for practicing solidarity this week.
- Reflect on the importance of putting solidarity into practice.
- Reflect on why solidarity is one of the pillars of Lovescaping.
- Take Action! Share how you practiced solidarity this week.

SOLIDARITY

DEFINITION

Solidarity is caring about the wellbeing of others and uniting to achieve a common goal. You are solidary when you give your time, support and care to others. When we are solidary, we support a cause even if it doesn't directly affect us. Solidarity is about realizing that we are all interconnected, so we stand together and support the wellbeing and liberation of others.

Examples of solidarity:

- ✓ You care about others.
- ✓ You volunteer and give your time to help.
- ✓ You support groups you are not a part of.
- ✓ You notice when someone is struggling and give your helping hand.
- ✓ You use your voice to provide support or assistance to people who need it.
- ✓ You believe we all have a responsibility to make sure everyone in our community is cared for.

Solidarity in Action

There are newly arrived refugees from Central America and Africa in your neighborhood. You say to your children: "Let's cook some food to welcome our new neighbors!" You prepare a delicious meal as a family and together go around the neighborhood delivering the food and welcoming the new neighbors.

IN YOUR OWN WORDS

How can you define **solidarity** in your own words?

_____
_____
_____
_____
_____
_____
_____

PRACTICE

Think of a situation in your own life where you can practice solidarity more intentionally. This can be a past experience where you didn't practice solidarity. How would you do it differently?

• What triggered you?	**What is the Lovescaping way?**
_____	_____
• How did you respond?	_____
_____	_____
• How did that response make you feel?	_____
_____	_____

GOAL SETTING

What is one SMART goal you will set this week to practice solidarity?

EXAMPLE:

This week, I will practice solidarity by volunteering at our local food bank with my children on Saturday morning and having a discussion with them about how we can more intentionally help the newly arrived immigrants in our neighborhood.

My goal for practicing solidarity this week:

_____
_____
_____

REFLECTION - SELF-EVALUATION

- Did you accomplish your goal/s?

- Why or why not?

- How will you continue practicing solidarity? What are your next steps? Write two actions for improving:

  1.

  2.

- Why do you think **solidarity** is one of the pillars of Lovescaping?

OBJECTIVES

LIBERATION

- Define liberation in your own words.
- Set a goal for practicing liberation this week.
- Reflect on the importance of putting liberation into practice.
- Reflect on why liberation is one of the pillars of Lovescaping.
- Take Action! Share how you practiced liberation this week.

DEFINITION

Liberation is the act of setting free. We practice liberation through our actions of love because we learn to respect each other's humanity. The act of loving is an act of freedom, because it has no boundaries, and it doesn't oppress or discriminate. Love liberates because it trusts, and it sets the people we love free. In the practice of love, we respect the individuality and freedom of every human being and we learn that our liberation is tied to each other's. Our liberation comes with great responsibility to practice it alongside the other pillars of Lovescaping so that we don't misuse it to harm others.

Examples of liberation:

- You are free to be yourself without pretending to be someone else.
- You want everyone to have the same rights.
- You speak up if you see an act of injustice.
- You believe everybody should be treated fairly.
- You are not jealous or possessive, instead you respect and trust.
- You do what you can to stop racism, discrimination, oppression, and all other forms of violence in the world.

Liberation in Action

Your daughter comes home and tells you that she overheard some kids at school making fun of a new student because she is a migrant. They were saying she doesn't belong here and should go back to her country. You tell her: "that's not acceptable. All individuals deserve equal treatment and respect, regardless of their background or origin. We need to speak up and educate others about the harmful effects of discrimination and prejudice. Let's talk to your school administration to ensure that they are taking appropriate measures to prevent and address such behavior."

IN YOUR OWN WORDS

How can you define **liberation** in your own words?

_____
_____
_____
_____
_____
_____
_____

PRACTICE

Think of a situation in your own life where you can practice liberation more intentionally. This can be a past experience where you didn't practice liberation. How would you do it differently?

- What triggered you?
  _____
- How did you respond?
  _____
- How did that response make you feel?
  _____

What is the Lovescaping way?
_____
_____
_____

GOAL SETTING

What is one SMART goal you will set this week to practice liberation?

EXAMPLE:

This week, I will practice liberation with my children by spending 15 minutes every night talking about who each one of us is. I will encourage them to think about what makes them unique and talk to them about the importance of our individuality, and feeling confident enough to be our true, authentic selves.

My goal for practicing liberation this week:

_____

_____

_____

REFLECTION - SELF-EVALUATION

- Did you accomplish your goal/s?

- Why or why not?

- How will you continue practicing liberation? What are your next steps? Write two actions for improving:

    1.

    2.

- Why do you think **liberation** is one of the pillars of Lovescaping?

OBJECTIVES

- Define gratitude in your own words.
- Set a goal for practicing gratitude this week.
- Reflect on the importance of putting gratitude into practice.
- Reflect on why gratitude is one of the pillars of Lovescaping.
- Take Action! Share how you practiced gratitude this week.

GRATITUDE

DEFINITION

Gratitude is a sense of thankfulness or appreciation for the good in our lives. To be grateful means to acknowledge other people's actions with kindness, to feel a sense of appreciation and thankfulness for what we are, for what we do, for what we receive and for what we have. It goes beyond saying "Thank you," to actually feeling it. When we start to acknowledge all the acts of kindness around us and to actively engage in reminding ourselves of everything that we can be grateful for, we begin to cultivate appreciation for our lives, for all the simple things that we often take for granted.

Examples of gratitude:

- ☑ You say thank you.
- ☑ You keep a gratitude journal.
- ☑ You look for the good in your life.
- ☑ You don't take things for granted.
- ☑ You don't compare yourself to others.
- ☑ You express gratitude regularly to people in your life.
- ☑ You notice all the small things in your life that you can be grateful for.
- ☑ You appreciate all the things others do for you.

Gratitude in Action

This past week your children have completed all the chores around the house. You decide to write them a thank you note to express how much you appreciate their work and how lucky you are to have them.

IN YOUR OWN WORDS

How can you define **gratitude** in your own words?

_____

_____

_____

_____

_____

_____

_____

PRACTICE

Think of a situation in your own life where you can practice gratitude more intentionally. This can be a past experience where you didn't practice gratitude. How would you do it differently?

- What triggered you?

  _____

- How did you respond?

  _____

- How did that response make you feel?

  _____

What is the Lovescaping way?

_____

_____

_____

_____

GOAL SETTING

What is one SMART goal you will set this week to practice gratitude?

EXAMPLE:

This week, I will practice gratitude every morning by thanking my children for small things that I tend to take for granted that I can start appreciating more.

My goal for practicing gratitude this week:

_____

_____

_____

REFLECTION - SELF-EVALUATION

- Did you accomplish your goal/s?

- Why or why not?

- How will you continue practicing gratitude? What are your next steps? Write two actions for improving:

    1.

    2.

- Why do you think **gratitude** is one of the pillars of Lovescaping?

OBJECTIVES

- Define forgiveness in your own words.
- Set a goal for practicing forgiveness this week.
- Reflect on the importance of putting forgiveness into practice.
- Reflect on why forgiveness is one of the pillars of Lovescaping.
- Take Action! Share how you practiced forgiveness this week.

FORGIVENESS

DEFINITION

Forgiveness is being able to let go of the negative emotions that someone or something made us feel, and finding peace within ourselves to forgive others. The process of forgiveness takes time, but in the end, it benefits us, since holding on to anger, resentment, and hatred will only cause us more pain. As imperfect human beings, we all make mistakes and we are all capable of hurting others, many times unintentionally. Being able to forgive others and asking for forgiveness are acts of love, and necessary ones if we want to nurture a relationship.

Examples of forgiveness:

- ☑ You are able to forgive others who have harmed you.
- ☑ You liberate yourself from negative emotions and find peace.
- ☑ You are able to ask for forgiveness when you have harmed someone (intentionally or unintentionally).
- ☑ You don't hold grudges.
- ☑ You don't seek revenge.
- ☑ You forgive but you don't forget.
- ☑ You know that forgiveness is a gift to yourself - it's not about the person who harmed you.

Forgiveness in Action

Your son has been suspended from school multiple times and you don't know what to do about it. You feel anger towards him because you think he's doing it on purpose. You have a heart to heart conversation with him where he opens up and reveals a challenge he's dealing with that you weren't aware of. He asks you to forgive him genuinely, stating that he wants to change. You forgive him and feel a huge weight has been lifted. You decide to help your son overcome his problem.

IN YOUR OWN WORDS

How can you define **forgiveness** in your own words?

_____
_____
_____
_____
_____
_____
_____

PRACTICE

Think of a situation in your own life where you can practice forgiveness more intentionally. This can be a past experience where you didn't practice forgiveness. How would you do it differently?

- What triggered you?
  _____
- How did you respond?
  _____
- How did that response make you feel?
  _____

What is the Lovescaping way?

_____
_____
_____

GOAL SETTING

What is one SMART goal you will set this week to practice forgiveness?

EXAMPLE:

This week, I will practice forgiveness by spending an hour over the weekend writing a letter to my sister asking for forgiveness for an incident that happened years ago that I never apologized for.

My goal for practicing forgiveness this week:

_____
_____
_____

REFLECTION - SELF-EVALUATION

- Did you accomplish your goal/s?

- Why or why not?

- How will you continue practicing forgiveness? What are your next steps? Write two actions for improving:

    1.

    2.

- Why do you think **forgiveness** is one of the pillars of Lovescaping?

OBJECTIVES

- *Define hope in your own words.*
- *Set a goal for practicing hope this week.*
- *Reflect on the importance of putting hope into practice.*
- *Reflect on why hope is one of the pillars of Lovescaping.*
- *Take Action! Share how you practiced hope this week.*

HOPE

DEFINITION

Hope is the guiding light that carries love through difficult and dark times. Hope means having faith in humanity and in the broader goal of creating a society based on the principles of love. It means believing that things will get better, that situations will improve, that change is possible. Hope is never lost in the pursuit of love, and it is the one pillar that can never, ever fall in our temple. Hope is always strong, holding the structure together and allowing us to rebuild the others.

Examples of hope:

- You believe that change is possible.
- You believe that you are capable of achieving your dreams.
- You persevere and know that situations can improve.
- You have an optimistic view of your future.
- You believe you are capable of overcoming obstacles.
- You give encouragement to others when they are feeling low.
- You see the light at the end of the tunnel.
- You don't give up.

Hope in Action

Your daughter wants to go to college. You don't have the means to pay for it but you are hopeful that you will find a way to help her achieve her goal. You begin to look up opportunities in community colleges and find scholarships she can apply to. You schedule a meeting with the school counselor to go over the best options with your daughter and actively encourage her every day to take action to fulfill her dream.

IN YOUR OWN WORDS

How can you define **hope** in your own words?

_____
_____
_____
_____
_____
_____
_____
_____

PRACTICE

Think of a situation in your own life where you can practice hope more intentionally. This can be a past experience where you didn't practice hope. How would you do it differently?

What triggered you?	**What is the Lovescaping way?**
How did you respond?	
How did that response make you feel?	

GOAL SETTING

What is one SMART goal you will set this week to practice hope?

EXAMPLE:

This week, I will practice hope with my family by spending 10 minutes every night writing down positive messages and affirmations that we can post around the house to give us encouragement and hope whenever we're feeling low.

My goal for practicing hope this week:

_____
_____
_____

REFLECTION - SELF-EVALUATION

- Did you accomplish your goal/s?

- Why or why not?

- How will you continue practicing hope? What are your next steps? Write two actions for improving:

   1.

   2.

- Why do you think **hope** is one of the pillars of Lovescaping?

FINAL REFLECTION

How has learning about the 15 pillars of Lovescaping impacted your definition and practice of love?

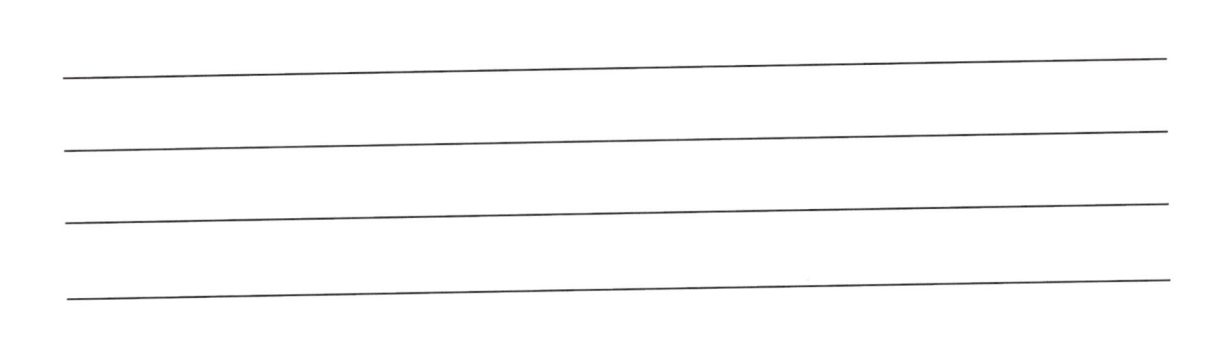

_____
_____
_____
_____

How do you think **hope** can help you rebuild the other pillars?

_____
_____
_____
_____

NOTES

NOTES

NOTES

NOTES

NOTES

NOTES

NOTES

Made in the USA
Columbia, SC
12 October 2024